I'M NOT SORRY
Poems by Cats

Rosa Silva

© 2018 Rosa Silva

ISBN-13: 978-1985123120
ISBN-10: 1985123126

Photos: cover design: Vanessa Mendozzi; page 5: Pexels/Janko Ferlic under a CC0 license; page 11: Rosa Silva; page 19: Pexels/John-Mark Smith under a CC0 license; page 25: Pexels/Ricardo Almagro under a CC0 license; page 31: Pexels/Monique Laats under a CC0 license; page 39: Pexels/Mustafa Ezz under a CC0 licence.

Contents

Mr. Fuzzybottom Stinkypants, The Third

The quatrain master

You can clean and clean…
and clean some more;
still you'll find cat hair everywhere,
even in your underwear.

There once was a mouse
and his name was Clause.
There once was a cat
who preferred to nap.

Here in your lap
is where I belong.
The fluff of your belly fat
is like a lullaby song.

My human does yoga
to deal with stress.
I just take a nap,
'cause I'm the fucking best.

My heart is red.
My eyes are blue.
If you try to pet me
I will bite you!

Stop looking for a mate
and just accept the fact
that your true soulmate
is me, your adorable cat!

The porcelain owl sat on a wall,
that stupid owl had a great fall.
Neither the cat lady nor the cat lady's man
couldn't put the owl together again.

The dog is a brainless thing
that cannot purr or climb or sing.
He barks all day long,
and thinks that makes him look strong.

There once was a pooch,
his name was Mooch.
There once was a pooch bed,
'cause I stole it they say I'm bad.

There once was a boyfriend
who came for the weekend.
He though he came to stay,
but I made him go away.

Petey O'Malley

*The most shameless
cat in the world*

You buy my favorite treats,
but you won't let me try your clean sheets.
You bring me catnip toys,
but you won't let me bite the boys.
You let me sleep on your lap,
but you'll interrupt my nap.
That's why I hate you and I love you…
That's why love you and I hate you…

One, two,
this kitty is going to get you.
Three, four,
don't even bother locking the door.
Five, six,
you won't be saved by the crucifix.
Seven, eight,
I'll keep you awake.
Nine, ten,
I'll never let you sleep again.

I roll over and offer you my tummy
because you're my human mommy.
I expose my fragile belly
which is as shaky as jelly.
I welcome the warm touch of your hand
and I feel like I'm in dreamland.
And then you pet me too hard
because I let down my guard.
And you still wonder why I attack
and bite your hand until it's black.

I lick, lick, lick, I lick my paw,
I clean every single claw.
I lick, lick, lick, I lick my tummy,
until it's as fluffy as a bunny.
I lick, lick, lick, I lick my tail,
until I feel like a proud male.
I lick, lick, lick, I lick my butt,
and then I lick your face.

I've scratched your comfortable couch,
and bit your hand 'till you said ouch.
I left paw marks on your newly-washed car,
and knocked off that beautiful cookie jar.
I brought a dead mouse inside the house,
and slept on your favorite blouse.
I attack your feet until they bruise.
No matter what I do I'm still your muse!
Human, you are a strange creature!

I like to sleep in the sink,
it's also a great place to have a drink.
But fresh laundry is the best,
when I sleep there I feel so blessed.
The linen closet is also good for a nap,
or even your comfortable lap.
With so many great places to sleep,
why did you buy me a bed that looks so cheap?

It's 6 a.m., it's time to eat.
It's 9 a.m., it's time for a treat.
It's 11 a.m., it's time for brunch.
It's 2 p.m., it's time for lunch.
It's 4 p.m., it's time for a snack.
It's 6 p.m., I could eat a macaque.
It's 8 p.m., it's time for dinner.
I'm sure this diet will make me thinner.

Let me in!
I felt so lonely out there.
Let me out!
Your presence is too much to bear.
Let me in!
The wind is chilling my ears.
Let me out!
It's feels like I've been here for years.

I brought you this present
and not a dollar I have spent!
I give you this little mouse
that I caught outside the house.
Oh, it seems I let him escape,
he hid under the drape.
Good luck catching that rat.
I would help if I didn't need to take a nap.

I can jump as high as eight feet,
and I always land on my feet.
My eyes can see in the dark,
I am as dangerous as a shark.
I am quiet and fast as a cheetah,
I am proud and fierce as a lion.
So, red dot, today is the day I'll catch you!

Snickerdoodle

The Haiku apprentice

New curtains.
Must attack right now.
Living room makeover.

Let me go outside.
It's cold. Let me back inside.
Indecisive? Not me.

Rub my belly!
Touch it and I'll shred your hand!
I changed my mind.

You are starving me.
Perhaps I'll barf on your shoe.
That will sure show you.

Untied shoe laces.
Must attack right now.
Best toy ever.

Fly on the windowsill.
Must climb onto the window and catch it.
After my nap.

I hate my new bed.
It's cold, hard and ugly.
Fruit bowl nap.

Dear toilet paper,
the battle is about to begin.
It's shredding time.

The world is waiting.
So much out there to explore.
Later. It's lunch time.

Glorious mornings.
It's 5 a-m. and time to play.
Wake up, wake up, wake up!

Junipurr

The sentimental

I meowed
as you
shut the door behind you

A long time ago
I had seven lives
now
I have only one left

I reached for the vase of flowers
one
two
three
four
I ate them

You are my human
I am your cat
we are one

If I am the longest relationship
of your life
it's time to
give me all the treats
and cuddling time
I am entitled to

Don't worry
don't cry
don't be disturbed
don't be annoyed
take a nap
life is too short

It's a blessing
to be a cat
do you know
how much humans love me

I meow to get your attention
look at me
play with me
pet me
I am your cat

Sometimes I love you
sometimes I hate you
sometimes I hate you and love you at the same time
I guess I'm human after all

Apologizing is
foreign to me
for I am a cat
and I'm always right

Muffin

The boss of the house

Welcome to my beautiful house,
this is my couch and this is my blouse.
Here's my King size bed,
and this is the toilet paper I like to shred.
This is the fruit bowl where I nap,
and this is my baseball cap.
Everything you see is mine,
including the human who drinks too much wine.

It's 10 a.m. and too soon to play.
It's 1 p.m. and time for the buffet.
It's 4 p.m. and time take a nap.
It's 6 p.m. and time to sit on your lap.
It's 3 a.m. and time to freak out,
to knock stuff over and yowl until I blackout.

You gave me a new bed,
I gave you a hairball straight from my gut.
You gave me yummy treats,
I let you smell my butt.
You gave me love and affection,
I unleashed my mighty claw.
You offered me your lap,
I showed you the power of the paw.
I am not sorry, for I am a cat,
Naughty and spoiled as a brat.

Fireworks give me a headache.
Honking car horns keep me awake.
Loud music makes me lazy.
The vacuum cleaner makes me crazy.
But do you know what really makes me mad?
Your high pitched voice which makes want to flee to
    Trinidad.

The best place to sit
is your favorite coat, I'll admit.
The preferred place to nap
is the sink and not your lap.
The freshest water in the club
comes from the bathtub.
Strange habits, you may say,
well, I just do it my way.

My cat lady Anna
looks just like a banana.
She bakes a yummy pie,
but she can't catch a fly.
She takes care of the house,
but she can't catch a mouse
That's why I am the master,
and she is just a disaster.

Get a dog
and you will find
troubles of every kind.
Get a dog
and I'll make him cry
until his brain begins to fry.

I hate the vet
and your other pet.
I hate your boyfriend
and your best friend.
I hate the dog
and the neighbors' bullfrog.
I hate you too
and I don't care if you're feeling blue.

I hear you calling me
but I don't care.
I don't mind your despair.
It's lunch time?
Then I'll be right there.
I wouldn't go elsewhere.

I don't like to brag,
but I can get inside any bag.
I don't like to boast,
but I always steal your toast.
I don't like to play my own trumpet,
but I manipulate you like a puppet.
That's why I am the cat
and you're my doormat.

Ms. Purrsnickitty

The Playful Kitty

Oops, I did it again,
I scratched the couch
and I clawed your pouch.
Oops, I did it again,
I stole your sock
and I knocked off the clock.
Oops, I will do it again
because this is my story
and I'm not sorry!

It's 6 a.m., time to wake up!
Look at my majestic butt.
I'll sit on your face
until you're awake.
I'll lick your hair
or I'll try the stare.
Wake up, wake up, it's a lovely day!
Wake up, wake up, it's time to play!

I jumped on the curtains
because I was trying to catch that fly.
I was so certain
I could tell that insect goodbye.

Red dot, red dot,
you'll be caught!
Red dot, red dot,
I'm planning a plot.
Red dot, red dot,
I hate you a lot.
Red dot, red dot,
You'll never be forgot.

O Christmas tree, o Christmas tree,
I want to play with your balls.
O Christmas tree, o Christmas tree,
I want to chew on your branches.
O Christmas tree, o Christmas tree,
I want to play with that topper.
O Christmas tree, o Christmas tree,
I climbed you like you're a wall.
O Christmas tree, o Christmas tree,
You and I had a great fall.

Little rat, little rat,
I threw you up in the air
and then you fell flat.
Little rat, little rat,
I let you escape
and now I don't know where you're at.

I knead my mommy,
I knead the blanket,
I knead the pillow,
and I'll knead you too.
That's why they call me the biscuit maker
and I don't mind 'cause I'm a proud baker.

Little tiny box,
let me get inside of you.
Little tiny box,
you know my love is true.
Little tiny box,
I know I can fit.
Little tiny box,
I'll just sit for a bit.

I like jumping on your back.
I love scratching your legs.
I like making biscuits on your lap.
I love licking your hair.
Dear human, you bring so much joy
'cause you're my human toy.

My litter box is always neat,
when I use it I'm so discreet.
The way the poop comes out of my bum
makes me feel completely numb.
When my business is finally done
it's time to have some fun.
I run as fast as I can.
I jump as high as I can.
This feels good, man!

12906845R00026

Printed in Great Britain
by Amazon